Hospitality Marketing Management

THIRD EDITION

Student Workbook

National Restaurant Association
EDUCATIONAL FOUNDATION

JOHN WILEY & SONS, INC.

New York • Chichester • Weinheim • Brisbane • Singapore • Toronto

ProMgmt. is a registered trademark of the National Restaurant Association Educational Foundation.

This student workbook is designed to be used with the textbook *Hospitality Marketing Management, Third Edition* by Robert D. Reid and David C. Bojanic.

This book is printed on acid-free paper.

Published by John Wiley & Sons, Inc.

Published simultaneously in Canada.

This publication is designed to provide accurate and authoritative information in regard to the subject matter covered. It is sold with the understanding that the publisher is not engaged in rendering professional services. If professional advice or other expert assistance is required, the services of a competent professional person should be sought.

Library of Congress Cataloging-in-Publication Data:

ISBN: 0-471-41309-7

Printed in the United States of America.

10 9 8 7 6 5 4 3 2 1

Contents

Introduction

Marketing is one of the most exciting and complex functions of a foodservice manager. By combining a knowledge of the market's behavior, a tailored product–service mix, and appropriate sales techniques, the foodservice marketing function represents one of your operation's best chances for success. Each of these three activities has its own set of steps crucial to your operation generating a satisfactory level of income. The purpose of this course is to introduce all aspects of the foodservice marketing function and to suggest ways you can apply it as a manager of your operation.

How to Earn a ProMgmt℠ Certificate of Course Completion

To earn a ProMgmt. Certificate of Course Completion, a student must complete all student workbook exercises and receive a passing score on the final examination.

To apply for the ProMgmt. Certificate of Course Completion, complete the student registration form located on the inside back cover of this workbook and give it to your instructor, who will then forward it to the National Restaurant Association Educational Foundation.

Each student registered with the Educational Foundation will receive a student number. Please make a record of it; this number will identify you during your present and future coursework with the Educational Foundation.

ProMgmt. certificate requirements are administered exclusively through colleges and other educational institutions that offer ProMgmt. courses and examinations.

If you are not currently enrolled in a ProMgmt. course and would like to earn a ProMgmt. certificate, please contact your local educational institution to see if they are willing to administer the ProMgmt. certificate requirements for non-enrolled students. You can also visit **www.edfound.org** for a list of ProMgmt. Partner schools. ProMgmt. Partner schools offer seven or more courses that include administration of the ProMgmt. certificate requirements.

The Educational Foundation leaves it to the discretion of each educational institution offering ProMgmt. courses to decide whether or not that institution will administer the ProMgmt. certificate requirements to non-enrolled students. If an institution does administer ProMgmt. certificate requirements to non-enrolled students, that institution may charge an additional fee, of an amount determined by that institution, for the administration of the ProMgmt. certificate requirements.

Course Materials

This course consists of the text *Hospitality Marketing Management, Third Edition,* by Robert D. Reid, the student workbook, and a final examination. The examination is the final section of your course and is sent to an instructor for administration, then returned to the Educational Foundation for grading.

Each lesson consists of:
- Student objectives
- Reading assignment
- Chapter exercises

At the end of the Workbook you will find:
- A study outline of the textbook
- A glossary (when the textbook does not have one)
- An 80-question practice test
- Answers to the practice test

The objectives indicate what you can expect to learn from the course, and are designed to help you organize your studying and concentrate on important topics and explanations. Refer to the objectives frequently to make sure you are meeting them.

The exercises help you check how well you've learned the concepts in each chapter. These will be graded by your instructor.

An 80-question practice test appears at the end of the workbook. All the questions are multiple-choice and have four possible answers. Circle the best answer to each question, as in this example:

Who was the first president of the United States?
- A. Thomas Jefferson.
- B. George Washington.
- C. Benjamin Franklin.
- D. John Adams.

Answers to the practice test follow in the workbook so that you may grade your own work.

The Final Exam

All examinations may first be graded by your instructor and then officially graded again by the Educational Foundation. If you do not receive a passing grade on the examination, you may request a retest. A retest fee will be charged for the second examination.

Study Tips

Since you have already demonstrated an interest in furthering your foodservice education by registering for this Educational Foundation course, you know that your next step is study preparation. We have included some specific study pointers that you may find useful.

- Build studying into your routine. If you hold a full-time job, you need to take a realistic approach to studying. Set aside a specific time and place to study, and stick to your routine as closely as possible. Your study area should have room for your course materials and any other necessary study aids. If possible, your area should be away from family traffic.

- Discuss with family members your study goals and your need for a quiet place and private time to work. They may want to help you draw up a study schedule that will be satisfactory to everyone.

- Keep a study log. You can record what lesson was worked on, a list of topics studied, the time you put in, and the dates you sent your exercises to your instructor for grading.

- Work at your own pace, but move ahead steadily. The following tips should help you get the most value from your lessons.

  1. Look over the objectives carefully. They list what you are expected to know for the examination.

  2. Read the chapters carefully, and don't hesitate to mark your text—it will help you later. Mark passages that seem especially important and those that seem difficult, as you may want to reread these later.

3. Try to read an entire chapter at a time. Even though more than one chapter may be assigned in a lesson, you may find you can carefully read only one chapter in a sitting.

4. When you have finished reading the chapter, go back and check the highlights and any notes you have made. These will help you review for the examination.

Reviewing for the Final Exam

When you have completed the final exercise and practice test, you will have several items to use for your examination review. If you have highlighted important points in the textbook, you can review them. If you have made notes in the margins, check them to be sure you have answered any questions that arose when you read the material. Reread certain sections if necessary. Finally, you should go over your exercises.

The ProMgmt. Program

The National Restaurant Association Educational Foundation's ProMgmt. Program is designed to provide foodservice students and professionals with a solid foundation of practical knowledge and information. Each course focuses on a specific management area. For more information on the program, please contact the National Restaurant Association Educational Foundation at 800.765.2122 (312.715.1010 in Chicagoland) or visit our web site at **www.edfound.org.**

Lesson 1

Student Objectives

After completing this lesson, you should be able to:

- Discuss various elements of the marketing environment.

- Explain the concepts of marketing and the marketing process.

- Define marketing mix and discuss how marketing programs are developed.

- Outline the difference between the terms *marketing* and *selling.*

- Discuss the role marketing plays in the management of a hospitality or travel firm.

- Explain the differences between the nature of products and the nature of services.

- Identify the reasons behind the growth in services.

- List attributes used to evaluate services.

- Explain the service quality process and identify potential gaps in service.

- Identify important issues in managing service.

- Explain the concept of customer satisfaction and how to assess it.

- Discuss why service failures occur and list what can be done to recover.

- Discuss service trends that will continue to affect the hospitality industry.

Reading Assignment

Now read Chapters 1 and 2 in the text. Use this information to answer the questions and activities in Exercises 1 and 2.

Chapter 1 Exercise

1. True (T) or false (F).

__F__ a. The major cause of employee turnover in restaurants is the number of working hours required.

__T__ b. In recent years, most of the growth in the hospitality industry has taken place in chain operations or the industry's corporate segment.

__F__ c. The product–service mix is the process of planning and executing the conception, pricing, promotion, and distribution of ideas, goods, and services to create exchanges that satisfy individual and organizational goals.

__T__ d. Nonprofit hospitality operations must be concerned with marketing.

__F__ e. The marketing mix is composed of price, product, place, promotion, and promise.

__T__ f. When a product or service is marketed in the proper manner, very little selling is necessary.

__T__ g. The key to successful marketing is trend recognition and the willingness to make necessary changes.

__T__ h. Word-of-mouth can be a very significant part of a company's promotional efforts.

2. How does the marketing mix for the hospitality industry differ from the traditional marketing mix?

   Some researchers believe that the traditional 4P's approach to the marketing mix does not apply to the hospitality industry.

3. Match each factor or situation with its external environment, using Economic (E), Social (S), Competitive (C), Political/Legal (P/L), or Technological (T).

   __C__ a. Price elasticity of demand

   __S__ b. Proportion of older Americans

   __P/L__ c. Changes in the federal tax codes

   __S__ d. Dietary habits of the American people

   __T__ e. Relational databases

   __E__ f. Consumer price index

   __T__ g. Resource management systems

   __C__ h. Oligopolies

   __E__ i. Variations in consumer purchasing power

   __P/L__ j. Tax credit for business meals and expenses

4. What are the three stages of the marketing management cycle?

- _marketing planning_
- _marketing execution_
- _marketing evaluation_

5. Which of the three questions asked during the marketing planning process is addressed by each task? Each number may be used more than once.

(1) Where are we now?

(2) Where do we want to go?

(3) How are we going to get there?

_1_ a. Examine past trends.

_2_ b. Set objectives for the future.

_3_ c. Devise strategies and action plans.

_2_ d. Make employees and stakeholders aware of the firm's strategic direction.

_3_ e. Develop marketing programs consistent with the firm's goals.

_3_ f. Ensure actions taken are integrated and lead to a common end.

_1_ g. Scan the environment.

_1_ h. Look for opportunities and threats.

_2_ i. Ensure goals are consistent with the firm's mission statement.

Chapter 2 Exercise

1. Below are nine reasons cited for the growth in services in recent years. Provide either a general or specific example illustrating each one.

- Changing patterns of government regulation

  The government has a less active role in the regulation of business activities.

- Relaxation of professional association standards market

  By letting the company ~~put~~ the product by any means necessary to get ahead.

- Privatization

  This transformation resulted in cost containment and a clearer focus on customer's needs.

- Computerization and technological innovation

  Feed back from customers on services. In powerment for the consumer.

- Growth in franchising

  Easier for someone to go to franchising than to start your own restaurant business.

- Expansion of leasing and rental businesses

  By leasing and renting has been a contributing factor in growth of the service sector.

- Manufacturers as service providers

  Profitable because services are provided.

- Market responses by nonbusiness organizations

  They look for ways to decrease cost and increase revenues.

- Globalization

<u>The trend in the service industry for firms to engage in more international commerce.</u>

2. Name five ways in which services differ from products.

- <u>greater involvement of customer in the production process</u>
- <u>People as part of the product.</u>
- <u>Difficulties in maintaing quality standards</u>
- <u>Absence of inventory</u>
- <u>Relative importance of the time factor</u>

3. Match each service-related term with its corresponding definition.

A (1) Service quality

B (2) Service gap

C (3) Communications gap

F (4) Knowledge gap

e (5) Service blueprint

D F (6) Standards gap

a. Perception resulting from attitudes formed by customers' long-term, overall evaluations of performance

b. Final difference between customers' expectations of a service and their perceptions of the actual service once it is consumed

c. Difference between management's perception of what customers expect and how they design the service delivery process to meet those expectations

d. Difference between service delivered and service promised

e. Flow chart that details the delivery process

f. Difference between management's perception of what consumers expect and consumers' actual expectations

4. What is the difference between the following?

   a.   Relationship marketing and internal marketing

Keeping exisiting customers.
Marketing to the employees.

   b.   System failures and customer needs failures

available services that becomes unavailable, system slow
or some other core service failure.
disputes between customer.

   c.   Comment cards and shopping reports

Comment card are left for customer to complete (Customer donot response
as much)
Secret shoppers. - results are more representative sample of
service expienerce.

5. Which five steps are required for improving customer service?

- Asses your current pthnation
- Degine your standards of qualityservice with measuable indicators
- Develope effective service improvement Strategy
- Initiate your solutions carefully.
- Provide feed back regognition and rewards

11

Lesson 2

Student Objectives

After completing this lesson, you should be able to:

- Identify external and internal factors that influence consumer decision making.

- Explain the process used by consumers to make purchase decisions.

- Explain alternate problem-solving processes and techniques.

- List some basic models of consumer behavior.

- Outline the differences between organizational and consumer buying processes.

- Define market segmentation.

- List variables commonly used to segment markets.

- Identify decisions that must be made when markets are segmented.

- Explain the connection between market segmentation decisions and development marketing strategies.

- Define positioning and explain its use in gaining a competitive advantage.

- Explain the relationship among market segmentation, targeting, and positioning.

Reading Assignment

Now read Chapters 3 and 4 in the text. Use this information to answer the questions and activities in Exercises 3 and 4.

Chapter 3 Exercise

1. To celebrate her promotion to advertising manager of a small public relations firm, Amanda is planning to take her department of five employees out to lunch. At the conclusion of a budget meeting, Amanda polls the group as to where the employees want to eat. Discuss how all six people's behavior might be influenced in this situation with respect to:

   a. Social setting

   b. Social forces

   c. Roles

   d. Attitudes relative to roles

   social setting make decisions and take action within the larger social setting and in doing so are influenced by their peers. Social forces - forces within the society set the standards of acceptable behavior. Role - is a pattern of behavior associated with a specific position within a social setting. Attitudes relative to roles attitudes and knowledge that we gain about the setting.

2. For each of these factors that influence consumer behavior:

   • Indicate whether it is an External (E) or Internal (I) influence, and

   • Provide an example.

   (1) Household

   • _E Parents decide when household is going out to_
   • _eat but children decide what restaurant will be visited_

   (2) Experience

   _I_ • _As the guest checks into hotel she is evaluating_
   • _the check in time base on her experience it will determine whether use the hotel again._

   (3) Socioeconomic level

   _E_ • _An upscale and expensive four ofive star resort property_
   • _will target its promotional efforts at those in upper income groups._

(4) Personal needs and motives

I • A consumer may have a need to dine out in
• order to enjoy a fine meal in as restaurant.

(5) Perception and attitude

I • Perception - low nutritional value poor culinary quality.
• Attitudes - attitudes about fast food high quality low cost

(6) Personality and self-image

I • Those in well define target market that are
• the most successful.

(7) Reference groups

E • When an individual peeks to become a member of a group
• his or her action are likely to emulate the group member behavior.

(8) Culture

E • In Europe its common to take 3 or more weeks of
• vacation in France the country could shut down
in the month of august.

3. A new Italian restaurant has opened its doors on the near north side. Which of the following groups should its marketing managers aim to reach? Circle all that apply.

a. Late majority d. Early majority

b. Laggards e. Early adopters

c. Innovators

4. Name the five major steps in the decision making process.

• Problem recognition
• Information search
• Evaluation and alternatives
• Purchase descion
• post purchase evaluation

16

5. Indicate the consumer problem-solving technique that applies to each item: Routine response behavior (R), Limited problem solving (L), or Extended problem solving (E).

    _E_ a. Products are high-priced and purchased infrequently.

    _R_ b. Consumers exert very little effort in the decision making process.

    _L_ c. There is some product differentiation.

    _L_ d. Customers are willing to exert some time and effort to ensure a good choice.

    _R_ e. Very little cognitive processing is required.

    _E_ f. Customers engage in an extensive search process.

    _E_ g. Customers evaluate alternative brands using many attributes.

    _R_ h. Hospital employees decide to eat lunch at the health care establishment's cafeteria.

6. How do organizational buyers differ from individual buyers?

Organizational buying process includes the stages used by organizations to determine needs search for information evaluate alternative make a purchase and evaluate the purchase. Individual is the same but for a single buyer.

Chapter 4 Exercise

True (T) or false (F).

_F_ 1. Market segmentation is used to separate the market into smaller heterogeneous groups.

_T_ 2. Segmentation can be used effectively by firms in the hospitality and travel industry.

_F_ 3. Firms must appeal to all potential customers.

_F_ 4. By segmenting the market, a firm will weaken its competitive position as well as its profits.

_T_ 5. There is a point at which a market can be segmented too much.

_T_ 6. When a firm segments a market, minimum cutoff points should be established relative to the size and projected demand of any segment.

_F_ 7. A Primary Metropolitan Statistical Area is the smallest urban area with an urban center population of 50,000 and a total metropolitan population of more than 100,000.

_F_ 8. The size of the average family has increased over the years.

_F_ 9. Life stages can be grouped under three overall categories: at-home singles, young couples, and empty nesters.

_T_ 10. Psychographics refers to segmentation based on lifestyle, attitudes, and personality.

_F_ 11. Psychographic statistics are used primarily to select the most effective advertising vehicles.

_F_ 12. Busy urbanites tend to discount health and nutrition considerations and recommendations.

_F_ 13. Behavioral variables allow management to segment the market based on benefits sought by consumers.

_T_ 14. The first step in the market segmentation process is to identify segmentation bases.

_F_ 15. Members of a selected target market should be those who place a high value on attributes the firm has used in its product–service mix.

_T_ 16. Projected demand can be defined as potential consumers having both purchasing power and motivation.

_F_ 17. Market share equals firm sales divided by total industry sales.

T 18. If consumers are alike and react in a similar fashion to components of the marketing program, a mass-market strategy should be used.

T 19. The overall objective of the differentiated strategy approach is to increase sales and market share by capturing sales from other big market segments.

T 20. A firm's *current* position is unimportant in positioning or repositioning the product–service mix.

T 21. In determining the ideal mix for consumers, firms must recognize price is not always the most important attribute.

T 22. In marketing, perceptions are everything.

T 23. A perceptual map is a graphic representation of how consumers in a market perceive a competing set of products relative to each other.

F 24. The easiest way to alter the marketing mix is to change the product–service mix.

T 25. The most successful firms tend to carve out a niche in the broad market.

Lesson 3

Student Objectives

After completing this lesson, you should be able to:

- Illustrate the need for marketing plans.

- Outline the differences between plans that have a strategic or tactical orientation.

- Discuss advantages and disadvantages of planning.

- Define terms such as *mission, goals and objectives, organizational resources, market risks and opportunities, evaluation plans, marketing strategies,* and *action plans.*

- List steps of the marketing planning process.

- Explain qualitative and quantitative techniques for developing sales forecasts.

- Identify components of a good marketing information system.

- List alternative sources of marketing information.

- Discuss the marketing research process and its role in collecting information.

- Highlight ethical issues surrounding marketing research and information systems.

Reading Assignment

Now read Chapters 5 and 6 in the text. Use this information to answer the questions and activities in Exercises 5 and 6.

Chapter 5 Exercise

1. What is the difference between each of the following?

    a.   Strategic planning and tactical marketing

    examination of a firm's core business strategy and primary marketing objectives

    b.   Goals and objectives

    Initial actions that will allow to achieve it stated goal long range, one year specific activities must be implemented.

2. Name the advantages and disadvantages of planning.

    Advantages

    - _& help firm cope with change more effectly_
    - _Helps ensure firm's objective achieve or modified._
    - _Aids in decision making_
    - _Firms operation (examine)_
    - _evaluation of marketing efforts._

    Disadvantages

    - _Time consuming_
    - _Support and commitment of topmgmt_
    - _poorly conceived / inacurate ineffective_
    - _short period / background work necessary_
    - _personnel and expertise._

    A. _tatical — focus on implementing the broad strategies that are established in the strategic plan._

3. Three newly promoted marketing managers from their respective Cozy Inn franchises met in early January to create a strategic marketing plan for their establishments. Diana, a recent college graduate with a background in finance, determined revenue goals for each franchise for the end of the calendar year. Based on these figures, Steve and Raoul created tentative budgets. Recognizing the continual increase in the proportion of older guests and rushed to develop a plan, the managers decided to focus on this segment.

Once a strategic plan had been established, each manager took it back to his or her franchise. Copies of the plan were made available to all employees, who were instructed to read the information and incorporate its suggestions into their day-to-day activities. At the end of the calendar year, profits, morale, and enthusiasm were all down.

Identify reasons the plan failed.

Financial projections was treated as marketing plan
Plans have to be implemented evaluated
and revised.
There is a lack of input from nonmarketing
Planning is based too heavily on short term result managers

4. Indicate the sequence of activities a firm should follow as it progresses through the marketing planning process, using the numbers 1 through 6.

   3   a. Conduct a situation analysis.

   2   b. Create a position statement.

   6   c. Implement marketing strategies and action plans.

   1   d. Establish a mission statement.

   4   e. Define the firm's goals and objectives.

5   **5**   f. Formulate marketing strategies and action plans.

5. Complete the following table.

Product Development Strategy Options

	New Product	Existing Product
New Market	market Penetration	Product Development
Existing Market	market Development	Product Diversification

6. Which five questions should information contained in action plans be able to answer?

- Who will assume primary responsibilities for each part of the action plan
- How they will proceed to implement the action plan
- Deadline when should they have it completed.
- What resource will be needed to fully implement a P
- what method and measures will be used to evaluate the plan.

7. What are the four key control areas used to evaluate performance?

- Sales control data.
- Cost control data
- Consumer feed back
- profit control data

8. Indicate whether each is a Qualitative (QL) or a Quantitative (QN) forecasting technique.

QL a. Expert opinion   QN e. Econometric models

QN b. Causal methods   QN f. Regression analysis

QL c. Delphi technique   QN g. Time series analysis

QL d. Sales force forecast   QL h. Survey of buying intentions

Chapter 6 Exercise

1. Match each marketing term with its corresponding definition.

_____(1) Secondary data

_____(2) Research design

_____(3) Sample

_____(4) Marketing information system

_____(5) Reliability

_____(6) Primary data

_____(7) Hypothesis

_____(8) Market research

_____(9) Sample unit

_____(10) Validity

a. Information collected for a specific reason or project

b. Information generated for a specific purpose when data is not available elsewhere

c. Basic level of investigation

d. Structure of people, equipment, and procedures used to gather, analyze, and distribute information needed by an organization

e. Statement indicating the relationship between or among two or more variables

f. Information previously collected for another purpose

g. Subset of the population

h. Accuracy of a measure

i. Consistency of responses to questions

j. Master plan specifying methods and procedures for collecting and analyzing needed information

2. To generate data beneficial to decision makers, a marketing information system should fulfill which three requirements?

- _____

- _____

- _____

3. Indicate which of the following are sources of Internal data (I) and which are sources of External data (E).

_____a. Management staff

_____b. Trade journals

_____c. University sources

_____d. Employees

_____e. Guest histories

_____f. Gallup polls

_____g. Convention and visitors bureaus

_____h. Sales data

4. What are the advantages and disadvantages of primary data?

_____

_____

_____

5. Which is descriptive research? Circle all that apply.

a. Experience surveys

b. Cross-sectional studies

c. Case analysis

d. Longitudinal studies

e. Causal research

f. Focus groups

6. Indicate which kind of survey applies to each, using T for telephone surveys, D for direct mail surveys, and P for personal interviews.

_____a. In-depth questioning

_____b. No face-to-face contact

_____c. Employee training required

_____d. Produce very quick results

_____e. High cost

_____f. Very slow data collection process

_____g. The most common method of survey data collection

_____h. Information not representative of the population

7. The following data were derived from a marketing research study: 600, 400, 600, 150, 750, 1,050, 200.

a.   What is the median?_____

b.   What is the mean? _____

c.   What is the range? _____

d.   What is the mode? _____

8. Which guidelines should be followed when preparing a final marketing research report?

_____

_____

_____

_____

Lesson 4

STRATEGIES FOR DEVELOPING AND MARKETING PRODUCTS AND SERVICES

Student Objectives

After completing this lesson, you should be able to:

- Explain the importance of developing product lines.

- Outline the process that many firms use to develop new products and services.

- List the various organizational structures that firms use to develop new products and services.

- Discuss the importance of brands, brand names, and trademarks.

- List the characteristics of effective branding.

- Discuss the four levels comprising the product–service mix.

- Define product life cycle and explain the role it plays in marketing strategy.

- Explain the wheel of retailing concept.

- Explain how to use a resource allocation model.

- Highlight issues surrounding managing services.

- Outline the role of distribution in hospitality and travel services.

- Discuss issues surrounding channel organization and management.

- List the types of intermediaries in the hospitality and travel industry.

- Discuss electronic commerce and its role in distribution.

Reading Assignment

Now read Chapters 7–9 in the text. Use this information to answer the questions and activities in Exercises 7–9.

Chapter 7 Exercise

1. Name three reasons a hospitality or travel firm should maintain a portfolio of products and services.

   - _____

   - _____

   - _____

2. For each strategy, indicate whether it is Reactive (R) or Proactive (P), and the type of strategy described.

   (1) Improves upon a competitor's product

   - _____

   (2) Determines customer wants and needs, then designs products and services to meet those needs

   - _____

   (3) Pools resources with another firm without combining ownership

   - _____

   (4) Counters effects on an existing product from a competitor's new product

   - _____

   (5) Searches for new ways to develop products and services

   - _____

   (6) Reacts to demands of customers

   - _____

   (7) Internally generates new ideas through means other than research and development

   - _____

   (8) Copies a new product or service before it can have a big impact in the market

   - _____

   (9) Acquires rights to new products or services by entering into a legal arrangement with another firm

   - _____

3. List and describe four organizational structures firms use to develop new products and services.

- _____
- _____
- _____
- _____

4. Donald Triumph owns The Hamburger Hut, a large quick-service establishment in the heart of a major city. Most of The Hut's customers are employees from surrounding businesses who come for lunch. In addition to hamburgers, the restaurant serves hot dogs and various chicken sandwiches. Donald wants to develop several new menu items, including gyros, meatball sandwiches, and several salad plates. Discuss the product development process he should go through before he offers any or all of these items on the menu.

_____

_____

_____

_____

_____

_____

5. What is the difference between a brand name and a brand mark?

_____

_____

Chapter 8 Exercise

1. Which are supporting products in the hotel industry? Circle all that apply.

   a. Concierge service

   b. Reservations departments

   c. Guest rooms

   d. Front desk personnel

   e. Shower facilities

   f. Twenty-four-hour room service

2. True (T) or false (F).

   _____a. Introduction stage goals are to develop product awareness and stimulate trial and adoption.

   _____b. Owners tend to attempt to standardize the physical plant during the growth stage.

   _____c. Profits tend to plummet during the maturity stage.

   _____d. The decline stage's major objectives are to increase overall marketing expenditures and decrease cash flow.

   _____e. Most products in the U.S. are in the maturity stage.

   _____f. A firm must often offer discounts and other promotions during the introduction stage.

   _____g. There is an increase in competitors during the growth stage.

   _____h. Customers tend to be early adopters during the introductory stage.

3. What are the seven steps in the product life cycle strategy development process?

   • _____

   • _____

   • _____

   • _____

   • _____

   • _____

   • _____

4. What can a marketing manager do by increasing sales to existing customers, increasing the number of users, and finding new uses for current products and services?

_____

_____

5. Classify each as a Star (S), Question mark (Q), Cash cow (C), or Dog (D).

_____a. Product with a low relative market share in an industry with high market growth

_____b. Product with low relative market share in an industry with low market growth

_____c. Self-sustaining products that don't require funds from other sources

_____d. Products used as sources of funds for SBUs in other categories

_____e. Product with high relative market share in an industry with high market growth

_____f. Product with high relative market share in an industry with low market growth

_____g. Products that drain the firm's resources and should be phased out or divested

_____h. Product that provides little or no positive cash flow and must be supported for growth or eliminated from the portfolio

6. Why do conflicts tend to arise between those responsible for sales and marketing and those with operational responsibilities?

_____

_____

7. Name three strategies for managing supply and demand.

- _____

- _____

- _____

Chapter 9 Exercise

1. Name and describe three channel width strategies.

   - _____

   - _____

   - _____

2. Match each term with its definition.

   _____(1) Convention and visitors' bureau

   _____(2) Authentication

   _____(3) Electronic commerce

   _____(4) Administered system

   _____(5) Legitimate power

   _____(6) Encryption

   _____(7) Franchising

   _____(8) Vertical marketing system

   a. Contractual agreement whereby one firm licenses a number of other firms to use its name and business practices.

   b. Result of contractual arrangements that specify channel members' expected behaviors.

   c. Security method requiring the use of some combination of account numbers, passwords, and IP addresses.

   d. Practice of carrying out business transactions over computer networks.

   e. System in which channel members work together as if they were one organization.

   f. Technique used to transform data to protect its meaning.

   g. System in which a manufacturer or supplier tries to control the flow of goods or services through a channel.

   h. Government-funded organization responsible for promoting a city or region.

3. Stella Smith has just become a franchisee of a national quick-service restaurant chain.

    a.   What advantages will she enjoy?

    b.   What disadvantages will she suffer?

    c.   What advantages will the franchisor enjoy?

    d.   What disadvantages will the franchisor suffer?

_____

_____

_____

_____

_____

_____

_____

_____

_____

_____

4. Provide three responsibilities of each intermediary.

    a.   Travel agents

- _____
- _____
- _____

    b.   Tour wholesalers and operators

- _____
- _____
- _____

    c.   Meeting planners

- _____
- _____
- _____

    d.   Hotel representatives

- _____
- _____
- _____

    e.   Travel bureaus

- _____
- _____
- _____

5. What is the difference between the Internet and the World Wide Web?

_____

_____

6. Name five ways hospitality and travel firms can use the Internet.

- _____

- _____

- _____

- _____

- _____

Lesson 5

PROMOTIONS, ADVERTISING, MERCHANDISING, AND PUBLIC RELATIONS

Student Objectives

After completing this lesson, you should be able to:

- Explain the difference between promotion and advertising.

- List elements of the promotional mix and discuss how they are managed.

- Explain how to establish promotional budgets.

- Outline the planning, creation, and evaluation of advertising campaigns.

- State the social consequences and economic effects of advertising.

- Explain the process of planning the media mix, including media selection and scheduling.

- Define terms and concepts used in the media planning process.

- List characteristics of various types of broadcast media.

- List characteristics of various types of print media.

- Discuss other forms of media used to support popular media vehicles.

- Explain the concept of sales promotions and its role in marketing strategy.

- List various types of sales promotions and the advantages and disadvantages associated with their use.

- Explain how to manage sales promotions.

- Discuss the concept of merchandising.

- Explain the concept of public relations and its role in marketing strategy.

- Outline various public relations techniques.

Reading Assignment

Now read Chapters 10–12 in the text. Use this information to answer the questions and activities in Exercises 10–12.

Chapter 10 Exercise

1. Which are elements of the promotional mix? Circle all that apply.

   a. Price

   b. Advertising

   c. Internet

   d. Place

   e. Public relations

   f. Sales promotion

   g. Personal selling

2. Name three functions of advertising and promotion.

   - _____

   - _____

   - _____

3. What is the main focus of the promotional campaign during each stage of the product life cycle?

   a. Introduction

   _____

   _____

   b. Growth

   _____

   _____

   c. Maturity

   _____

   _____

   d. Decline

   _____

   _____

4. What is the difference between a fixed budget and a contingency budget?

_____

_____

5. The Hospitality Hotel will be opening its doors at the end of the month. To develop an advertising and promotion budget, the hotel's managers have conducted extensive research about what similar hotels in the area are spending. They have decided to base their budget on the industry average. Which budget method are they employing?

_____

6. When developing the theme for an advertising campaign, which four checkpoints should be considered?

- _____   - _____

- _____   - _____

7. Complete the model.

Advertising Planning

	Organizational Objectives			

Chapter 11 Exercise

1. True (T) or false (F).

_____a. Good media objectives are stated in general, nontechnical language.

_____b. Advertising is just one part of the total marketing mix.

_____c. Flighting media schedules provide a constant low-level flow of advertising with intermittent periods of blitz advertising.

_____d. Local advertising campaigns should be distinct from national advertising efforts.

_____e. A medium should be selected based on its ability to reach the maximum number of potential consumers at the lowest C.P.M.

_____f. If high-income households are exposed to ads for luxury hotels, the result is wasted coverage.

_____g. Stages in the media planning process are similar to those in the marketing planning process.

2. Fill in the table by listing at least two advantages and two disadvantages for each medium.

Medium	Advantages	Disadvantages
Radio		
Direct mail		
Newspapers		
Television		
Magazines		

3. Indicate whether each is a Print Advertising term (P) or a Broadcast Media term (B).

_____a. C.P.M.

_____b. Circulation

_____c. Drive time

_____d. Preemptible rates

_____e. Dubbing

_____f. Milline formula

_____g. Reach

_____h. Fade in/fade out

_____i. Agate line

_____j. Prime time

_____k. Gross rating points

_____l. Fringe time

_____m. Bleed

4. Indicate whether each guideline applies to Print (P), Radio (R), Television (T), or Outdoor (O) advertising.

_____a. Mention the name of the hospitality operation and the benefit early on.

_____b. Make the print large.

_____c. Keep the message simple and straightforward.

_____d. Don't include the hospitality operation's telephone number or hours of operation.

_____e. Suggest immediate action.

_____f. Capture consumer attention immediately.

_____g. If an advertisement has been effective, repeat it.

_____h. Use a maximum of five to seven words.

_____i. Attract consumer attention with a headline.

_____j. Write copy that makes consumers visualize products and services.

_____k. Use coupons.

5. What do the letters AIDA, as used in direct mail advertising, stand for?

_____

_____

6. Which media are considered support media?

_____

_____

Chapter 12 Exercise

1. Sales promotion is typically used to accomplish which objectives? Circle all that apply.

   a. To stimulate demand during peak periods

   b. To help managers determine the appropriate media mix

   c. To increase consumer awareness

   d. To encourage current customers to purchase less

   e. To ensure job security for managers and salespeople alike

   f. To combat competition

2. Identify each as a push or a pull technique.

   _____a. Sampling

   _____b. Cooperative advertising

   _____c. Sweepstakes

   _____d. Price reduction coupons

   _____e. Electronic collateral material

   _____f. Conventions and managers' meetings

   _____g. Contests

   _____h. Premiums

   _____i. Point-of-sale displays

   _____j. Combination offers (bundling)

   _____k. Price reduction promotions

   _____l. Advertising materials

3. What are the differences among a contest, a sweepstakes, and a lottery?

   _____

   _____

   _____

4. Sequentially order these steps to successful promotion. Use the numbers 1 through 11, with 1 indicating the first step and 11 the last.

_____Brainstorm about the potential offer.

_____Develop an implementation timetable.

_____Develop the promotional budget.

_____Select the promotional technique.

_____Establish specific objectives.

_____Conduct internal training of the entire staff.

_____Select the target market.

_____Create the promotional theme.

_____Select the advertising media and support vehicles.

_____Monitor results.

_____Work the plan.

5. Name five ways to effectively suggestive sell.

- _____

- _____

- _____

- _____

- _____

6. Match each aspect of training guest-contact and service personnel with its "technical" category. Some numbered items may be used more than once.

_____a. product–service knowledge

_____b. Attitude

_____c. Reassurance

_____d. Physical skills

(1) Psychomotor aspect

(2) Affective aspect

(3) Cognitive aspect

7. Which is a commonly used public relations technique? Circle all that apply.

a.   House newsletter

b.   Photographs

c.   Sampling

d.   Posters

e.   Open houses

f.   Speeches

Lesson 6

PERSONAL SELLING, PRICING STRATEGY, AND MENU DESIGN

Student Objectives

After completing this lesson, you should be able to:

- Outline the fundamentals of selling and the profiles of successful salespeople.

- List the basic markets for hotel group sales and identify their decision factors.

- Explain the personal selling process and its role in promotion.

- Discuss the art of negotiating and key account management.

- Outline the ethical issues of personal selling.

- Discuss the meaning of price and its use in strategic marketing.

- Explain the effect of pricing objectives, consumer price sensitivity, and the external environment on pricing decisions.

- Outline broad pricing strategies that can be used by a firm based on the relationship between price and economic value.

- Discuss the use of price in segmenting consumer markets.

- Explain the relationship among cost, price, demand, and the basic pricing techniques.

- List legal and ethical issues surrounding pricing decisions.

- Explain the importance of menus in foodservice marketing.

- List guidelines used in selecting and categorizing menu items.

- Outline the process for designing and producing actual menus.

- Identify potential pitfalls associated with menu planning.

- Discuss methods and guidelines used in evaluating menus.

Reading Assignment

Now read Chapters 13–15 in the text. Use this information to answer the questions and activities in Exercises 13–15.

Chapter 13 Exercise

1. What is the difference between an order taker and an order getter?

   _____

   _____

2. List five characteristics of a successful salesperson.

   • _____

   • _____

   • _____

   • _____

   • _____

3. What do the letters *F*, *A*, and *B* stand for in the FAB selling technique? Why are these words used?

   _____

   _____

4. For each, provide two examples of questions a meeting planner might ask.

    a.   Location

        • _____

        • _____

    b.   Professional service

        • _____

        • _____

    c.   Adaptability and flexibility

        • _____

        • _____

    d.   Cost

        • _____

        • _____

5. Is each type of meeting typically conducted by a member of the Association market (A) or the Corporate market (C)?

    _____a. New product introduction meetings

    _____b. Annual stockholders' meetings

    _____c. Management meetings

    _____d. Committee meetings

    _____e. Board of directors meetings

    _____f. Seminars and workshops

    _____g. Technical meetings

    _____h. Training meetings

    _____i. Annual conventions for entire membership

    _____j. Sales meetings

6. What are four steps in the personal selling process?

- _____
- _____
- _____
- _____

7. Most objections fall into which categories? Circle all that apply.

a. Company

b. Lack of need

c. Price

d. Pressure to decide

e. Ethics

f. Product

8. In the following scenario, which method is Stuart the salesperson using to handle Cora the meeting planner's objection?

Cora: The Royal Hotel quoted me only $10,000 for the same package.

Stuart: While the Royal Hotel does charge the same price, the employee-to-guest ratio there is 60 to 1. We offer a ratio of 40 to 1. We also offer attendees access to our Olympic-size pool and our health club facility. And attendees can use the banquet hall for a full five hours.

_____

9. Name three specific examples of unethical behavior among salespeople.

- _____
- _____
- _____

Chapter 14 Exercise

1. What are four types of pricing objectives?

- _____

- _____

- _____

- _____

2. Match each effect with its corresponding definition.

_____a. Shared cost

_____b. Expenditure

_____c. Perceived substitutes

_____d. Price-quality

_____e. End benefit

_____f. Difficult comparison

_____g. Unique value

(1) Consumers will be more sensitive the higher a product's price is relative to the prices of perceived substitutes for the product.

(2) Consumers may be aware of substitutes for a product, but will tend to be less price sensitive the more difficult it is to compare brands.

(3) Consumers will be less sensitive to a product's price to the extent they believe higher prices signify higher quality.

(4) Consumers will be less sensitive to a product's price when the product is unique and doesn't have close substitutes.

(5) The more price sensitive a firm's consumers are, the more price sensitive the firm will be in purchasing components of the end benefit.

(6) Consumers will be more sensitive to a product's price the higher the amount of the total cost.

(7) Consumers will be less sensitive to a product's price if another organization or individual is sharing in the cost of the product.

3. What are the differences among skim pricing, penetration pricing, and neutral pricing?

_____

_____

_____

_____

4. Which is an equation for break-even in units? Circle all that apply.
   a. BEP = Total fixed costs/(Selling price + Variable cost)
   b. BEP = [Total fixed costs/(Selling price − Variable cost)] 3 Selling price
   c. BEP = Total fixed costs/Contribution margin
   d. BEP = Total fixed costs/Total variable costs
   e. BEP = (Selling price − Variable cost)/Total fixed costs

5. What is the price elasticity of demand?

_____

_____

6. Name six ways to price by segment and provide one example of each.
   • _____
   • _____
   • _____
   • _____
   • _____
   • _____

7. When is a price ethical?

_____

_____

Chapter 15 Exercise

1. True (T) or false (F).

_____a. A detailed sales history is not valuable in menu planning.

_____b. One of the menu's main goals is to encourage new patrons to come to the establishment.

_____c. Modifications in the kitchen layout may be necessary to facilitate production of new menu items.

_____d. Every effort should be made to provide consumers with the option of a meal that will satisfy two-thirds of the recommended dietary allowance.

_____e. Menu census data is published by the federal government in an effort to regulate the foodservice industry.

_____f. The menu is one of the best ways a foodservice establishment can communicate with customers.

_____g. Menus must be balanced.

_____h. The menu should contribute to establishing the operation's perceived image.

_____i. Signature items should be heavily promoted on the menu.

2. Which is commonly used to disguise menu price increases? Circle all that apply.

a.   Portions are traded off with price changes.

b.   Prices are listed in a straight line.

c.   Prices are raised when a new menu is introduced.

d.   Price increases are made across the board.

e.   Prices are crossed out or written over.

f.   Odd-even pricing is used.

3. Oliver the owner has created a new menu for his Italian restaurant. On the cover he has included a photograph of the building, its name, and the restaurant's logo. In an effort to focus customers' attention on entrées, he has listed them first, followed by drinks, appetizers, soups, salads, and desserts. Since Oliver is so proud of all of his offerings, he has given them equal attention on the menu. However, he has positioned first those items that are least popular so customers may be induced to select them. Oliver has so many food items to list that he has used 7-point type so he can fit everything in. Even so, he doesn't have room to include a description of each item. He has therefore put all type in capital letters so it will stand out, despite its size.

Identify problems with Oliver's new menu.

_____

_____

_____

_____

4. Name three factors that should be considered when designing a wine list.

- _____

- _____

- _____

5. For each area, provide one example of possible inaccurate representation on a menu.

   a. Quantity

   _____

   b. Quality

   _____

   c. Price

   _____

   d. Brand names

   _____

   e. Product identification

   _____

   f. Point of origin

   _____

   g. Merchandising terms

   _____

   h. Means of preservation

   _____

   i. Food preparation method

   _____

   j. Verbal and visual presentation

   _____

   k. Nutritional claims

   _____

6. Match each description or example with its corresponding type of cycle. Each number may be used more than once.

(1) Typical cycle menu

(2) Typical break cycle menu

(3) Random cycle menu

_____a. Used for extended "captive" customers.

_____b. Begins on the same day.

_____c. Each menu is assigned a letter, letters are picked at random, and then assigned to individual days.

_____d. Thursday is spaghetti day.

_____e. Begins each new cycle on a different day.

7. Name three approaches to menu evaluation.

- _____

- _____

- _____

Study Outline

Chapter 1

1. Marketing is the process of planning and executing the conception, pricing, promotion, and distribution of ideas, goods, and services to create exchanges that satisfy individual and organizational goals.
2. Companies that use the **marketing concept** determine customer wants and needs, then design products and services that meet those wants and needs, while at the same time meeting the firm's goals.
3. The traditional **marketing mix** is composed of 4Ps: price, product, place, and promotion.
4. The **product–service mix** is composed of all the tangible and intangible products and services that make up a hospitality operation.
5. The marketing mix modified for the hospitality industry includes the product–service mix, presentation mix, and communication mix.
6. Marketing managers must monitor changes in five external environments: economic, social, competitive, political/legal, and technological.
7. In marketing a hospitality operation, management activities are divided into three major areas: marketing planning, marketing execution, and marketing evaluation.
8. Three basic questions should be addressed during the marketing planning process.
    *   Where are we now?
    *   Where do we want to go?
    *   How are we going to get there?
9. Management must integrate and monitor its key result areas, including operations, finance, human resource management, and research and development.

Chapter 2

1. Strategies that have been used for product marketers do not always work successfully for those who market services.

2. Several factors have contributed to the substantial growth of services.
   - Changing patterns of government regulation
   - Relaxation of professional association standards
   - Privatization
   - Computerization and technological innovation
   - Growth in franchising
   - Expansion of leasing and rental businesses
   - Manufacturers as service providers
   - Market responses by nonbusiness organizations
   - Globalization
3. There are six key differences between services and products.
   - Customers of services are involved in the production of services.
   - Those who purchase services come in contact with other consumers as well as service employees.
   - It is impossible to control the quality of services in the same way as the quality of manufactured products.
   - Services can't be inventoried for future use.
   - Hospitality services are usually produced and consumed simultaneously.
   - The distribution channel for services is usually more direct than the traditional channel used by many product firms.
4. The service quality process is the product of the expectations and perceptions of a firm's management, its employees, and the customers it serves.
   - Whenever there are differences in expectations or perceptions, there is a potential for a gap in service quality.
   - To provide high-quality service, all staff members must view the guest as the highest priority.
5. **Customer satisfaction** occurs when a firm's service meets or exceeds customers' expectations.
6. Improving customer satisfaction should be a top priority of all managers working in the hospitality industry.

7. The process for improving customer service includes five steps.

   (1) Define your own standards of quality service with measurable indicators.

   (2) Assess your current situation.

   (3) Develop effective service improvement strategies.

   (4) Initiate your solutions carefully.

   (5) Provide feedback, recognition, and rewards.

8. Commonly-used techniques for assessing customer satisfaction include spoken comments and complaints, surveys and comment cards, number of repeat customers, trends in sales and market share, and shopping reports.

9. Issues and trends critical to understanding hospitality and tourism marketing include shrinking customer loyalty, increasing consumer sophistication, and increased emphasis on the needs of individual customers.

Chapter 3

1. The study of consumer behavior focuses on understanding consumers as they purchase products or services.

2. Human behavior is influenced by a variety of factors including the social setting, social forces, roles, and attitudes relative to roles.

   - External factors that influence consumer behavior include culture, socioeconomic level, reference groups, and household.

   - Internal factors that influence consumer behavior include personal needs and motives, experience, personality and self-image, and perception and attitude.

   - Maslow's five identified needs, arranged in the following hierarchy: physiological, safety, social and belonging, esteem, and self-actualization.

3. People can be classified according to their willingness to change as innovators, early adopters, early majority, late majority, or laggards.

4. The consumer decision making model is composed of five steps.
   (1) Problem recognition
   (2) Information search
   (3) Evaluation of alternatives
   (4) Purchase decision
   (5) Post-purchase evaluation

5. Consumers use both compensatory and noncompensatory processes to integrate information they have obtained over time to evaluate and choose among various alternatives.
   - The three noncompensatory strategies are conjunctive, disjunctive, and lexicographic.

6. Consumer problem-solving techniques might be routine response behavior, limited problem solving, or extended problem solving.

7. Organizational buyers differ from individual buyers in a variety of ways.
   - Organization buyers usually purchase in large volumes.
   - Demand for organization products is derived from the demand for consumer products.
   - Products in organization markets tend to be more technical in nature.
   - Organization buyers tend to be professionals with extensive knowledge of the product.
   - Organizations tend to become repeat purchasers.
   - More than one person is often involved in the organizational buying process.

8. Five specific roles identified for people constituting a buying unit are the user, influencer, buyer, decider, and gatekeeper.

Chapter 4

1. **Market segmentation** means to pursue a marketing strategy such that the total potential market is divided into homogenous subsets of customers, each of which responds differently to the organization's marketing mix.

2. Market segmentation can improve sales and profits because it allows the targeting of specific market segments that are most likely to patronize the organization's facilities.

3. Three criteria used to evaluate the effectiveness of a market segmentation strategy are substantiality, measurability, and accessibility.

4. Marketing managers can use **geographic, demographic, psychographic, behavioral, and benefits sought** variables when segmenting consumer markets.

5. There are four steps in the market segmentation decision process.

   (1) Identify segmentation bases.

   (2) Develop profiles for each segment.

   (3) Forecast demand.

   (4) Select specific target market segments.

6. Once specific target markets have been identified, three segmentation strategies can be applied: mass market, differentiated, or concentrated.

7. **Positioning** is the process of determining how to differentiate, in the minds of consumers, a firm's product offerings from those of its competitors.

8. There are four steps in the positioning process.

   (1) Determine the ideal mix for consumers.

   (2) Measure consumer perceptions of available services.

   (3) Look for gaps in coverage and select a desired position.

   (4) Develop a strategy for obtaining the desired position.

Chapter 5

1. **Strategic planning** is the process of determining a firm's primary goals and objectives and initiating actions that allow the firm to achieve these stated goals and objectives.

2. **Tactical marketing** plans focus on implementing broad strategies established in the strategic plan.

3. Marketing plans help firms cope with changes, ensure objectives are achieved or modified, help managers make decisions, force them to examine the firms' operations, and help managers evaluate marketing efforts.

4. There are several reasons that strategic plans might fail.
   - They are not integrated into a firm's daily activities.
   - Those responsible for planning don't understand the planning process.
   - There is a lack of input from nonmarketing managers.
   - Financial projections are treated as marketing plans.
   - There is insufficient consideration of all environmental variables.
   - Planning is based on short-term results.
   - There are no procedures established to monitor and control the planning process.
5. The **mission statement** defines the purpose of the firm and how it attempts to differentiate itself from its competitors.
6. The marketing planning process includes four steps.
   (1) Conduct a situation analysis.
   (2) Define the firm's goals and objectives.
   (3) Formulate marketing strategies and action plans.
   (4) Implement action plans and monitor performance.
7. Sales forecasting techniques can be separated into two categories: qualitative and quantitative.
   - Qualitative forecasting techniques include expert opinion, the Delphi technique, sales force forecasts, and surveys of buying intentions.
   - Quantitative forecasting techniques include time series analysis, causal methods, regression analysis, and econometric models.
8. In selecting a forecasting technique, management should consider the time horizon, availability of data, pattern of data, desired level of accuracy, cost, and ease of application.

Chapter 6

1. A **marketing information system** is the structure of people, equipment, and procedures used to gather, analyze, and distribute information needed by an organization.
2. Market research is information collected for a specific reason or project.
3. A successful marketing information system should be objective, systematic, and useful.
4. Having accurate information is key to an effective marketing information system.

5. Information sources can be grouped into two main categories: secondary and primary.

- Secondary data have been previously collected for another purpose.
- Primary data are generated for a specific purpose when the information is not available elsewhere.
- All data can be derived from internal or external sources.
- Managers should perform a secondary data search before collecting primary data.

6. There are five steps in the marketing research process.

(1) Define the problem.

(2) Plan the research.

(3) Collect the data.

(4) Analyze the data.

(5) Prepare the final report.

7. **Research design** is the master plan specifying methods and procedures for collecting and analyzing needed information.

- The three main categories of research design are exploratory, descriptive, and causal.

8. The three possible methods for obtaining primary data are observation, surveys, and experiments.

9. A **population** is the entire target market that is being studied; a **sample** is a subset of the population.

10. The two basic forms of statistical analysis used in marketing research are **descriptive** and **inferential.**

11. In preparing the final report, the marketing researcher should consider the audience, understand the needs of the audience, and anticipate and address possible objections and concerns.

12. **Research ethics** are the codes of behavior set by society and the research industry to define appropriate behavior for firms and individuals.

Chapter 7

1. Product development takes two forms: **innovation** and **follow the leader.**

2. Hospitality and travel firms can benefit from a portfolio of products in several ways.

   - Diversifies a firm's operating risk
   - Provides growth opportunities for the firm
   - Allows for the efficient and effective use of a company's resources
   - Increases a company's market share and its importance within the overall market

3. **Reactive** strategies for new product development include **defensive, imitative, second but better,** and **responsive.**

4. **Proactive** strategies include **research and development, marketing, entrepreneurial, acquisition,** and **alliance.**

5. Firms use a variety of organizational structures for new product planning, including new product committees, new product departments, product managers, and venture teams.

6. The new product development process consists of five stages.

   (1) Idea generation

   (2) Product screening

   (3) Concept testing

   (4) Business analysis and test marketing

   (5) Market introduction

7. Brands can help firms increase sales, profitability, and customer satisfaction.

   - A **brand** is the name, sign symbol, design, or any combination of these items used to identify the product and establish an identity unique from those of competitors.
   - Brand names should be easy to pronounce, recognize, and remember; describe the benefits of the product or service; be translatable into foreign languages; and be distinctive and capable of legal protection.

Chapter 8

1. Four basic product levels are the **core product, facilitating products, supporting products,** and **augmented products.**

2. The four phases of the product life cycle are introduction, growth, maturity, and decline.

3. To develop strategies for the product life cycle, managers should follow a seven-step process.

   (1) Compile historical data.

   (2) Identify competitive trends.

   (3) Determine changes in the product–service mix.

   (4) Study the product life cycles of similar products.

   (5) Project sales.

   (6) Locate the product's current position in the life cycle.

   (7) Begin strategy formulation.

4. Marketing managers can extend the product life cycle by increasing sales to existing customers, increasing the number of users, and finding new uses for existing products.

5. The **wheel of retailing** is founded on the notion that retail firms that enter the low end of the market with basic products and low prices tend to gravitate toward the high end of the market.

6. Firms should view themselves as a portfolio of products that both provides funds and needs funds.

   - Within the portfolio are brands of items referred to as **strategic business units (SBUs).**

7. The **Boston Consulting Group (BCG) matrix** classifies products and services according to their relative market share and the market growth rate of the industries they are in.

   - **Question marks** have low relative market share in industries with high market growth.
   - **Stars** have high relative market share in industries with high market growth.
   - **Cash cows** have high relative market share in industries with low market growth.
   - **Dogs** have low relative market share in industries with low market growth.

8. Within any service industry, there are often conflicts between those responsible for sales and marketing and those with operational responsibilities.

   - Sales and marketing personnel attempt to do everything to increase revenue.
   - Operations personnel aim to increase efficiency and reduce costs.

9. Managers in different functional areas can be persuaded to work together in five ways.

    (1) Transferring managers across functional areas

    (2) Creating cross-functional teams

    (3) Cross-training associates to perform a broader variety of tasks

    (4) Delegating authority to individual units

    (5) Instituting gain-sharing programs

10. Strategies to manage supply and demand include:

    - Modify price.

    - Develop programs to boost nonpeak demand periods.

    - Shift demand through reservations.

    - Increase personnel efficiency.

    - Increase consumer involvement in self-service aspects of the service delivery system.

Chapter 9

1. A firm's distribution strategy must be consistent with other elements of its marketing mix.

2. The main objective of the distribution function is to get products and services to consumers where, when, and how they prefer them.

3. The **channel width** decision is based on the desired amount of market coverage. The **channel length** decision is based on the number of intermediaries between a manufacturer and the final consumer.

4. **Channel power** is the ability of one channel member to influence the behavior of other channel members in such a way as to get them to do things they ordinarily would not do.

5. In a **vertical marketing system,** channel members work together as if they were one organization.

6. Franchising is a contractual arrangement whereby one firm (the franchisor) licenses a number of other firms (the franchisees) to use the franchisor's name and business practices.

7. The hospitality and travel industries use a variety of intermediaries.
   - Travel agents are responsible for a large volume of bookings for airlines, hotels, and cruises.
   - Tour wholesalers and operators obtain services that can be combined in a package and offered to the leisure market.
   - Meeting planners negotiate with hotels, airlines, and other travel firms on behalf of their members for guest rooms and meeting space.
   - Hotel representatives are responsible for selling guest rooms and meeting space to groups.
   - Travel bureaus are responsible for promoting a state or region as a travel destination.
8. Electronic commerce, primarily the **Internet,** allows business to be transacted over computer networks in an effort to improve organizational performance.
9. Hospitality and travel firms use web sites to provide customer service, sell products or services, educate and inform potential customers, offer discounts, promote products, improve brand image, obtain customer information, and build databases.

Chapter 10

1. Advertising and promotion present information to consumers and reinforce consumer behavior by communicating with people who have patronized a particular organization.
   - Advertising also induces first-time patronage and enhances the image of hospitality operations.
2. Advertising should establish awareness and positive value in the minds of consumers and promote repeat patronage and brand loyalty among customers.
3. One component of the marketing mix that changes over the life cycle of a product is promotion.
4. Promotional budgets force managers to look into the future, serve as reference points, and foster improved communication among individuals creating such budgets.
5. Budgeting methods include **percentage of sales, desired objective, competitive parity,** and **all-you-can-afford.**
6. Advertising is defined as any paid form of nonpersonal presentation and promotion of ideas, goods, or services by an identified sponsor.

7. A successful advertising campaign strategy revolves around objectives, the targeted audience, key consumer benefits, support, and tone and manner.

8. When developing the theme for an advertising campaign, the advertiser must check for maintenance of visual similarity, verbal similarity, similarity of sound, and similarity of attitude.

9. Five components of the advertising planning model are input from the marketing information system, organizational objectives, planning and strategy formulation, implementation, and evaluation of advertising effectiveness.

10. Commonly used techniques for evaluating an advertising campaign include copy testing, inquiry and sales, coupons and split runs, sales tests, and consumer testing of awareness, recall, and attitude.

11. An advertising agency can increase advertising's effectiveness, overcome special production requirements of radio and television advertising, maintain close contacts with media representatives, and offer consulting services.

12. Advertising has both strong proponents and harsh critics.

Chapter 11

1. Four steps comprise the media planning process.

   (1) Conduct market analysis.

   (2) Establish media objectives.

   (3) Develop media strategies to attain objectives.

   (4) Evaluate the program on a continual basis.

2. To develop media strategies, a firm must select the media mix, determine target market and geographic coverage, and schedule media.

3. Print media include newspapers, magazines, and phone directory ads.

4. Techniques for successful print advertising include:

   - Attract the consumer's attention with the headline.

   - Include visual components.

   - Keep the layout and copy simple and straightforward.

   - Use coupons.

   - When a print advertisement has been effective, don't hesitate to repeat it.

5. Broadcast media are distributed over airwaves, allowing consumers to be passive listeners.

   • Among these media are radio, television, and the Internet.

6. Techniques for successful radio advertising include:

   • Commercials should be kept fairly simple.

   • Music and lyrics should be simple.

   • Ads should suggest immediate action.

   • Ads should speak directly to consumers.

   • Copy should be written so listeners can visualize the products and services.

7. Television advertising techniques include:

   • Show people in the actual setting.

   • Capture the viewer's attention immediately.

   • Stay with one idea and repeat it within the allocated time.

   • Accurately project the firm's image.

8. Six types of television commercials are: demonstration, straight announcer, testimonial, problem solving, story line, and musical.

9. A tried-and-true approach to direct mail advertising is based on AIDA (attention, interest, desire, action).

10. Support media include outdoor advertising, brochures, and collateral materials.

Chapter 12

1. Sales promotions seek to increase consumer awareness, introduce new products and services, increase customer counts, combat competition, encourage present consumers to purchase more, and stimulate demand in nonpeak periods.

2. Push promotions encourage increased purchases and increased consumption by consumers.

   • Push techniques include point-of-sale displays, cooperative advertising, advertising material, traditional and electronic collateral material, conventions, and managers' meetings.

3. Pull promotions are aimed at stimulating the interest of consumers and having them pull the product through channels of distribution.

   - Pull techniques include sampling, price reduction promotions and coupons, combination offers or bundling, premiums, contests, and sweepstakes.

4. Coupons stimulate trial of a product or service by reducing its price, encouraging multiple purchases, and generating temporary sales increases.

5. The primary objective of sampling is to encourage trial of new products.

6. Premiums are used to bring in new customers, encourage more frequent visits by current customers, and build positive word-of-mouth about the firm.

7. Contests and sweepstakes are designed to increase the number of customers and build market share, often at the expense of the competition.

8. For successful promotions, management must perform the following steps:

   - Select the target market for the promotion.
   - Establish specific objectives for the promotion.
   - Select the promotional technique.
   - Brainstorm about the potential offer.
   - Create the promotional theme.
   - Develop the promotional budget.
   - Select the advertising media and vehicles to support the promotion.
   - Develop an implementation timetable.
   - Conduct internal training of the entire staff.
   - Work the plan.
   - Monitor results.

9. Service people are salespeople and must be trained to suggestive sell, increase check averages, deliver additional profits, and ensure guest satisfaction.

10. The basic aspects of training guest-contact and service personnel are product–service knowledge, physical skills, attitude, and reassurance.

11. Public relations is the process by which relationships with various constituencies are managed.

12. Common public relations techniques include news releases, photographs, letters, inserts, enclosures, house organs and newsletters, speeches and public appearances, posters, bulletin boards, exhibits, audio-visual materials, and open houses and tours.

Chapter 13

1. Successful salespeople are courteous, have complete knowledge of the product–service mix being sold, behave professionally, have a desire and willingness to work, are organized, and have strong personalities.
2. **Meeting planners** plan meetings to be attended by all sorts of individuals.
3. In the **FAB selling technique,** salespeople relate a product's benefits to the consumer's needs by stressing its features and advantages, thereby selling benefits.
4. Most meeting planners must focus on cost, location, image and status, professional service, adaptability and flexibility, and professional operations and management.
5. Three main categories of the meetings market are association meetings, conventions and trade shows, and corporate meetings.
6. Personal selling is an interpersonal process whereby the seller ascertains, activates, and satisfies the needs and wants of the buyer so that both seller and buyer benefit.
7. The personal selling process includes prospecting and qualifying, planning and delivering sales presentations, overcoming objections, and closing the sale.
8. Salespeople must be ready to negotiate with buyers.
9. Common types of unethical behavior among salespeople include sharing confidential information, reciprocity, bribery, gift giving, making misleading sales claims, and business defamation.

Chapter 14

1. Pricing is a continual process that requires a firm grasp of the market and its environments.
2. There are four major categories of pricing objectives: financial performance, volume, competition, and image.

3. The most common effects on consumer price sensitivity include:
   - Price-quality effect: Consumers will be less sensitive to a product's price to the extent they believe higher prices signify higher quality.
   - Unique value effect: Consumers will be less price sensitive when a product is unique and doesn't have close substitutes.
   - Perceived substitutes effect: Consumers will be more price sensitive the higher a product's price is relative to the prices of perceived substitutes.
   - Difficult comparison effect: Consumers will tend to be less price sensitive the more difficult it is to compare brands.
   - Shared cost effect: Consumers will be less price sensitive if another organization or individual is sharing in the cost of a product.
   - Expenditure effect: Consumers will tend to be more price sensitive the larger the amount of the total expenditure.
   - End benefit effect: The more price sensitive the firm's consumers are, the more price sensitive the firm will be in purchasing components of the end benefit.
4. Developments in a firm's economic, social, political, technological, and competitive environments can affect the firm's pricing decisions.
5. A firm can adopt any number of pricing strategies, including skim pricing, penetration pricing, and neutral pricing.
   - In skim pricing, prices are set high in relation to the product's or service's economic value to most potential consumers.
   - In penetration pricing, prices are set low in relation to the firm's economic value to most potential consumers.
   - The neutral pricing strategy involves setting prices at a moderate level.
6. Three pricing techniques firms can use for products and services are cost-oriented, demand-oriented, and competitive.
   - Cost-oriented pricing includes **break-even analysis, cost-plus pricing,** and **target-return pricing.**
   - Demand-oriented approaches use consumer perceptions of value as a basis for setting prices.
   - Competitive pricing emphasizes price in relation to direct competition.
7. Segmented pricing can be done by buyer identification, purchase location, time of purchase, purchase volume, product design, or product bundling.

8. Pricing practices are illegal if they are anticompetitive or if they take unfair advantage of consumers.

Chapter 15

1. A successful menu should further the marketing concept's goals, contribute to establishing the operation's perceived image, act as a means to influence customer demand for menu items, and help an operation gain a competitive advantage.

2. Improvements in computer technology have had a great effect on the restaurant industry with respect to menu design and printing.

3. During the initial stages of the menu design process, factors that should be considered are the consumer, the operation's sales history, the skills of production and service employees, the physical layout and design of the operation, recommended daily allowances, menu balancing, and menu census data.

4. One of the most critical decisions facing restaurant managers is raising menu prices.

    • The less attention drawn to a price increase, the better.

5. The menu cover should include the restaurant name and logo and reflect the operation's theme and atmosphere.

6. When listing menu items, they should appear in the same order in which the customer will eat them. Not all items should receive equal attention on the menu; those that are most popular and most profitable should be seen first by the consumer. Items should be described, not merely listed.

7. When designing a wine list, foodservice managers should link specific wines with individual entrees on the menu and provide a description of the wine on the actual wine list.

9. Menus should be the right physical size, feature type large enough to be readable, include descriptive selling copy, and avoid using tacky clip-ons.

10. All representations in menus must be accurate.

11. Cycle menus are used by institutional operations to keep menus from being monotonous.

12. Menus can be evaluated by counting the number of times each item is sold, comparing sales figures to regional and national data, or by performing menu engineering analysis.

Practice Test

This Practice Test contains 80 multiple-choice questions that are similar in content and format to those found on The Educational Foundation's final examination for this course. Mark the best answer to each question by circling the appropriate letter. Answers to the Practice Test are on page 95 of this Student Workbook.

Lesson 1: Introduction to Hospitality Marketing

1. Which is considered a service?
   A. Meal purchased at a quick-service restaurant
   B. Plant purchased from a commercial greenhouse
   C. Child's toy purchased from a discount retail chain
   D. Computer purchased from an electronics superstore

2. The four Ps of marketing are
   A. promise, proffer, persuade, push.
   B. pick, price, product, place.
   C. price, product, place, promotion.
   D. price, promise, place, persuade.

3. Selling focuses primarily on a firm's desire to
   A. respond to customers' needs.
   B. eliminate the competition.
   C. satisfy its sales staff.
   D. sell products for revenue.

4. The element a marketing manager uses to increase the tangibility of the product–service mix is known as
   A. market segmentation.
   B. distribution.
   C. the presentation mix.
   D. promotion.

5. Which of the following exists among companies that make the same class of products?
   A. Price elasticity of demand
   B. Product category competition
   C. Monopolistic competition
   D. Bartering

6. In marketing a hospitality operation, management activities can be divided into which three major areas?
   A. Marketing planning, marketing execution, and marketing evaluation
   B. Operations, finance, and human resource management
   C. Pricing, placing, and promoting
   D. Presenting, communicating, and distributing

7. A contractual arrangement whereby one firm licenses a number of other firms to use its name and business practices is called
   A. product bundling.
   B. discretionary effort.
   C. franchising.
   D. boundary spanning.

8. Since consumers tend to be present when a service is provided within a hospitality operation, they are
   A. chronic complainers.
   B. sophisticated.
   C. involved in the service production.
   D. often dissatisfied.

9. Attributes consumers can investigate prior to making purchase decisions are called
   A. experience qualities.
   B. credence qualities.
   C. service qualities.
   D. search qualities.

10. To develop a service quality orientation, customers should be perceived as
    A. the lifeblood of every business.
    B. dependent on the hospitality business.
    C. outsiders.
    D. owners.

11. Pay raises and bonuses are examples of
    A. extrinsic rewards.
    B. convivial dimension.
    C. critical incidents.
    D. moments of truth.

12. Which of the following is a short-term strategy that seldom builds brand loyalty?
    A. Branding
    B. Price discounting
    C. Relationship marketing
    D. Empowerment

Lesson 2: The Hospitality Consumer Market

13. Consumer behavior tends to be
    A. chaotic.
    B. rational and predictable.
    C. highly variable.
    D. influenced by the consumer price index.

14. The dominant culture in the United States today stresses
    A. frugality.
    B. individualism.
    C. nationalism.
    D. privacy.

15. In the typical household, leadership is often
    A. delegated.
    B. absent.
    C. shared.
    D. a point of contention.

16. The process by which stimuli are recognized, received, and interpreted is known as
    A. perception.
    B. attitude.
    C. adoption.
    D. diffusion.

17. During post-purchase evaluation, a consumer who is having second thoughts may be experiencing
    A. Maslow's hierarchy of needs.
    B. a critical moment.
    C. the reality effect.
    D. cognitive dissonance.

18. People who have authority to select or approve a supplier on behalf of their organization are called
    A. deciders.
    B. influencers.
    C. approvers.
    D. buyers.

19. The three criteria that should be used to evaluate the effectiveness of any market segmentation strategy are
    A. substantiality, measurability, and accessibility.
    B. geography, behavior, and benefits sought.
    C. MSA, PMSA, and CMA.
    D. revenue, profit, and satisfaction.

20. Chicago, Los Angeles, and New York are examples of
    A. Primary Metropolitan Statistical Areas.
    B. segmentation by city.
    C. demographics.
    D. attribute data.

21. Married parents whose children are adults who have moved out are categorized as
    A. empty nesters.
    B. Baby Boomers.
    C. retirees.
    D. mature parents.

22. The objective of identifying segmentation bases is to
    A. match the stated wants and needs of the targeted segment with the product–service mix offerings and marketing communications of the firm.
    B. determine the similarities and differences among and between various target markets.
    C. develop a homogenous market segment made up of consumers who will respond in a similar manner to marketing strategies and communications efforts.
    D. initiate the market segmentation process.

23. Firms that appeal to more than one market segment with a separate marketing program for each segment use which of the following market segmentation strategies?
    A. Mass-market
    B. Concentrated
    C. Combination
    D. Differentiated

24. Perceptual mapping can be used
    A. to determine the physical layout of a proposed hospitality firm.
    B. to learn about consumers' desires and how these are or are not satisfied by current products and services in the market.
    C. by operations managers in the daily supervision of a firm.
    D. to establish some unique element of the product–service mix.

Lesson 3: Marketing Plans and Marketing Information

25. Which of the following answers the question, "What business are we in?"
    A. Position statement
    B. Goal
    C. Mission statement
    D. Objective

26. The letters in S.W.O.T. analysis stand for
    A. Seek, Wait, Obligate, Test.
    B. Strengths, Weaknesses, Opportunities, Threats.
    C. Strategic Window Opens Today.
    D. Stability, Wisdom, Opportunity, Time.

27. What is a potential problem with a firm having multiple objectives?
    A. Additional staff might need to be hired to accomplish the objectives.
    B. There might be a conflict between the objectives.
    C. The product–service mix will probably have to be altered.
    D. There are no problems associated with having multiple objectives.

28. Which product development strategy is commonly used during periods of inflation?
    A. Market development
    B. Market penetration
    C. Product development
    D. Product diversification

29. Which forecasting technique is most appropriate when only historical sales data is available?
    A. Time series analysis
    B. Expert opinion
    C. Regression analysis
    D. Econometric models

30. The ongoing data-gathering process is known as
    A. marketing research.
    B. inferential analysis.
    C. a marketing information system.
    D. exploratory research.

31. Information that was previously collected for another purpose is called
    A. primary information.
    B. past information.
    C. secondary information.
    D. beta-test information.

32. Which of the following is a source of internal marketing information?
    A. Trade associations
    B. Syndicated services
    C. Internet
    D. Guest histories

33. Before collecting primary data, managers should
    A. perform a secondary data search.
    B. consult with top management.
    C. establish a marketing research budget.
    D. re-evaluate the market research problem to be investigated.

34. Which of the following measures a population at one point in time?
    A. Focus group
    B. Cross-sectional study
    C. Telephone survey
    D. Longitudinal study

35. "Are you planning to purchase a mini-van within the next six months?" is an example of a(n)

A. open-ended question.
B. dichotomous question.
C. multiple category question.
D. leading question.

Lesson 4: Strategies for Developing and Marketing Products and Services

36. Product development can take which two forms?

A. Innovation and follow-the-leader
B. Diversification and product lines
C. Acquisitions and alliances
D. Research and development

37. The larger the portfolio of products and product lines, the smaller a firm's

A. budget.
B. diversification.
C. business risk.
D. profits.

38. Which reactive strategy is characterized by responding to and improving upon a competitor's new product?

A. Defensive
B. Imitative
C. Second but better
D. Responsive

39. Instead of combining ownership, some firms choose to form

A. alliances.
B. committees.
C. departments.
D. venture teams.

40. The final stage of the product development process is

A. concept testing.
B. idea generation.
C. business analysis and test marketing.
D. market introduction.

41. A symbol or logo design used to identify a product is called a

A. brand.
B. brand mark.
C. trademark.
D. character.

42. Additional goods and services that can be bundled with core products in an attempt to increase overall value for consumers are called

A. peripheral services.
B. facilitating products.
C. supporting products.
D. managing services.

43. Which product life cycle stage is associated with rapidly rising sales and a decreasing cost per unit?

A. Introduction
B. Growth
C. Maturity
D. Decline

44. Reducing overall marketing expenditures and increasing cash flow during the decline stage is a strategy known as

A. milking the brand.
B. demand shifting.
C. ARGE.
D. product–service mix differentiation.

45. Promoting baking soda for use as a refrigerator deodorizer is an example of which strategy for extending the product life cycle?

A. Increasing sales to existing customers
B. Finding new uses
C. Increasing the number of users
D. Increasing sales through advertising

46. The wheel of retailing is founded on the idea that retail firms which enter the low end of the market with basic products and low prices tend to

A. go out of business quickly.
B. go directly from the growth stage to the decline stage of the product life cycle.
C. move locations frequently.
D. gravitate toward the high end of the market.

47. Products and services that have low relative market shares in industries with high market growth rates are called

A. dogs.
B. cash cows.
C. question marks.
D. stars.

48. The channel width decision is based on the

A. expertise of the channel members.
B. nature of the industry.
C. desired amount of market coverage.
D. number of intermediaries between the manufacturer and the final consumer.

49. Referent power occurs when one channel member
    A. has prestige that might benefit another member as a result of their association.
    B. is able to influence the behavior of another member through the use of incentives.
    C. is able to influence another channel member's behavior through the use of threats.
    D. has superior knowledge relative to another channel member.

50. The package concept is particularly appealing to
    A. domestic travelers.
    B. seniors.
    C. experienced travelers.
    D. individual travelers.

51. Which of the following acts as a clearinghouse for information regarding large meetings, conferences, and conventions?
    A. Travel agents
    B. Internet
    C. Hotel representatives
    D. Convention and visitors' bureaus

52. Which of the following improves security in electronic commerce?
    A. Cyberspace
    B. Hypertext
    C. Firewall
    D. Browser

Lesson 5: Promotions, Advertising, Merchandising, and Public Relations

53. One component of the marketing mix that changes over the life cycle of a product is
    A. promotion.
    B. product.
    C. place.
    D. promise.

54. A firm should use its competitive advantage to launch new products and services that will further strengthen the organization during which stage of the product life cycle?
    A. Introduction
    B. Growth
    C. Maturity
    D. Decline

55. After paying its expenses, Roadside Inn considers the allocation of resources to promotion and advertising. What kind of budgeting method does the firm use?

A. Percentage of sales
B. All-you-can-afford
C. Desired objective
D. Competitive parity

56. Any promotion that is not paid for is called

A. a freebie.
B. advertising.
C. publicity.
D. sponsorship.

57. Advertising objectives focus on

A. market share.
B. producing a specified percentage of increase in sales volume or a specified percentage of increase in repeat patronage.
C. the selection of individual media.
D. increasing consumer awareness and drawing consumers away from the competition.

58. Periods of blitz advertising, with no advertising between blitzes, is called

A. flighting media.
B. continuous advertising.
C. pulsing advertising.
D. reach scheduling.

59. Which of the following is a disadvantage of radio advertising?

A. Clutter
B. Long lead time for ad placement
C. High absolute cost
D. Low selectivity

60. A television commercial featuring satisfied customers talking about elements of the product–service mix is called

A. demonstration.
B. testimonial.
C. story line.
D. straight announcer.

61. The AIDA principle is a tried-and-true approach to

A. newspaper advertising.
B. direct mail advertising.
C. radio advertising.
D. billboard advertising.

62. Blank boards on which a printed ad is mounted are known as

A. painted bulletins.
B. posters.
C. collateral materials.
D. specialty advertising.

63. Which sales promotion approach encourages increased purchases and increased consumption by consumers?

A. Push
B. Pull
C. Cooperative
D. Traditional

64. Winning which is based solely on chance?

A. Contests
B. Sweepstakes
C. Premiums
D. Sampling

65. Which aspect of guest-contact and service personnel training is not easily taught or changed?

A. Product–service knowledge
B. Physical skills
C. Attitude
D. Reassurance

66. A fact sheet and a biographical sketch of the general manager are usually parts of an organization's

A. collateral package.
B. point-of-sale display.
C. premium offer.
D. press kit.

67. Which should be routinely sent to the media as part of an organization's public relations effort?

A. Photographs
B. House organs
C. News releases
D. Posters

Lesson 6: Personal Selling, Pricing Strategy, and Menu Design

68. Targeting specific groups of consumers within a condensed time frame is known as

A. SMERF.
B. telemarketing.
C. sales blitzing.
D. negotiation.

69. The FAB selling technique focuses on

A. family, acceptance, and brands.
B. freedom, action, and belongings.
C. functions, alternatives, and buildings.
D. features, advantages, and benefits.

70. Which is characteristic of the association market?

A. Small meeting size
B. Short decision making process
C. Narrow market
D. Long lead times for planning

71. Which is critical to successful selling?

    A. Active listening
    B. Ability to overcome objections
    C. Negotiation
    D. Ethics

72. Which pricing objectives focus on a firm's overall positioning strategy?

    A. Volume
    B. Image
    C. Financial performance
    D. Competition

73. The higher a product's price relative to the prices of perceived substitutes for the product,

    A. the less price sensitive consumers will be.
    B. the more price sensitive consumers will be.
    C. the more likely consumers will be to buy the product.
    D. the less likely consumers will be to buy the product.

74. The cost of a competing product consumers perceive as the closest substitute is known as the product's

    A. economic value.
    B. differentiation value.
    C. reference value.
    D. financial value.

75. If fixed costs associated with a hospitality product are $800, selling price is $35 per unit, and variable cost is $25 per unit, what is the break-even point in dollars?

    A. $80
    B. $1,650
    C. $2,100
    D. $2,800

76. The percentage change in quantity demanded divided by the percentage change in price is known as

    A. price elasticity of demand.
    B. prestige pricing.
    C. the law of demand.
    D. price lining.

77. Selected menu items for which a foodservice establishment is noted are called

    A. clip-ons.
    B. signature items.
    C. special.
    D. RDAs.

78. Items having ingredients that fluctuate greatly in cost should be

    A. listed as "market price" on the menu.
    B. priced on the menu.
    C. listed in a prominent place on the menu.
    D. excluded from the menu entirely.

79. The random cycle menu is used for
    A. quick-service customers.
    B. uninformed customers.
    C. corporate customers.
    D. extended "captive" customers.

80. The simplest way to evaluate menus is
    A. through menu engineering.
    B. by counting the number of times each item is sold.
    C. by comparing sales figures to regional and national data.
    D. by plotting menu items on a sales mix analysis matrix.

Practice Test Answers and Text Page References